THE PAINT BOOK

BY HANNAH TOFTS
Written and Edited by Diane James
Photography by Jon Barnes

CONTENTS

SIMON AND SCHUSTER BOOKS FOR YOUNG READERS

Simon & Schuster Building, Rockefeller Center, 1230 Avenue of the Americas, New York, New York 10020

Text and compilation copyright © 1989 by Two-Can Publishing Ltd. Illustration and design copyright © 1989 by Hannah Tofts. All rights reserved including the right of reproduction in whole or in part in any form. Originally published in Great Britain by Two-Can Publishing Ltd. First U.S. edition 1990. SIMON AND SCHUSTER BOOKS FOR YOUNG READERS is a trademark of Simon & Schuster Inc. Manufactured in Portugal.

10 9 8 7 6 5 4 3 2 1   (pbk.) 10 9 8 7 6 5 4 3 2 1

Library of Congress Cataloging-in-Publication Data: Tofts, Hannah.   The paint book / by Hannah Tofts ; written and edited by Diane James ; photography by Jon Barnes.— 1st U.S. ed. Summary: Describes and illustrates a variety of painting techniques, including wax and paint, stenciling, glass painting, and face painting. 1. Art—Technique—Juvenile literature. [1. Art—Technique.] I. James, Diane. II. Barnes, Jon ill. III. Title N7433.T6 1990 89-21893 751—dc20 CIP AC ISBN 0-671-70364-1   ISBN 0-671-70365-X (pbk.)

All of the things on these pages are used somewhere in the PAINT book. You should be able to find most of them in your house or at school but some you may have to buy from craft stores or toy stores.

Keep a lookout for things that might be useful – plastic spoons, plastic and aluminum foil containers, and scraps of fabric.

For most painting you can use poster or tempera paints. But for some things you will need special paints.

It is useful to have a selection of fat and thin brushes – short, stiff brushes are good for stenciling and spattering.

Some painting can be extremely messy so keep a good supply of newspaper to put on the floor.

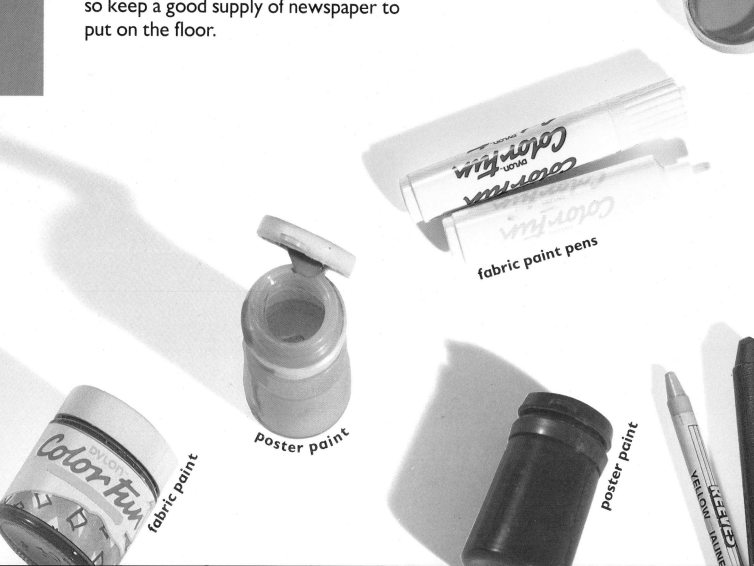

colored candles

fabric paint pens

poster paint

fabric paint

poster paint

fabric for decorating

straws for spattering

small brushes

large pointed brush

fabric paint

large flat brush

WHISTLER 65

stencil brushes

egg for decorating

string for printing

WINSOR & NEWTON · ENGLAND

wax crayons

Mixing your own colors can be very satisfying. Although you may get muddy colors sometimes, they will certainly be different!

Try adding more and less water when you are mixing paints to give different effects.

Color Mixing
Yellow + Red = Orange
Blue + Yellow = Green
Blue + Red = Purple

Look around the house for empty yogurt containers, plastic trays, and lids to mix paints in.

Keep your eyes open for useful brushes such as old toothbrushes, small scrubbing brushes, and paint brushes.
If no one wants them, you can cut them down and use them for stenciling or spattering.

Try not to damage your brushes by being rough with them when you are mixing. Moving them in just one direction will keep the hairs smooth and make the brushes last longer.

HANDS AND FEET

All the family can join in the fun of hand and feet painting! First, put down plenty of newspaper because it can be very messy!

Cover the bottoms of your feet with fairly thick paint and make footprints on a large sheet of paper. You should get an interesting effect and the paint will wash off afterwards.

After a bit of practice, try making patterns using both hands and feet. It is best if one person is in charge of directing the others!

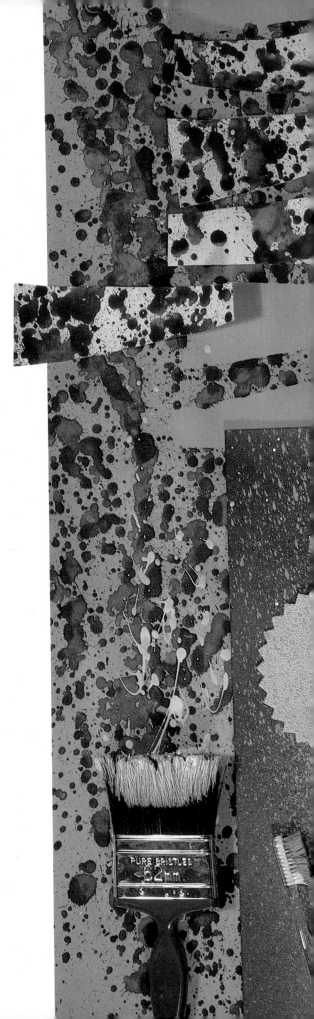

Straw Painting

Drip some runny paint onto a sheet of paper. Get close to the paint and blow gently through a straw. The paint should make strange patterns as it spreads across the paper.

If you add a second color right away, the colors will mix and blend together in places. If you don't want this effect, wait until the first color is dry.

Spatter With Small Brushes

Find a selection of small brushes with short, stiff bristles, such as old toothbrushes or nailbrushes. Dip one of the brushes in medium thick paint. Hold the brush over a large sheet of paper and run a small piece of cardboard down the bristles. You should get a fine speckled effect on the paper!

Try masking out areas by laying shapes of cardboard on the clean paper. Spatter over the shapes. When you lift off the cardboard, there will be a clear shape left behind!

Spatter With Large Brushes

Find the kind of paint brush normally used to paint walls. Cover it with medium thick paint. Stand over a large sheet of paper and flick the brush up and down. You should get an interesting effect of large speckles! Try using different colors on top of each other.

All of these methods are very messy so make sure all surfaces are well covered.

▼ Fold a large sheet of paper in half. Unfold the paper and drop some fairly runny paint along the fold and on either side of the fold. Fold the paper over along the original fold and smooth it over with your hand. You can use just one color or several different colors. If you don't want the colors to run together, allow each color to dry before you drop on blobs of the next color.

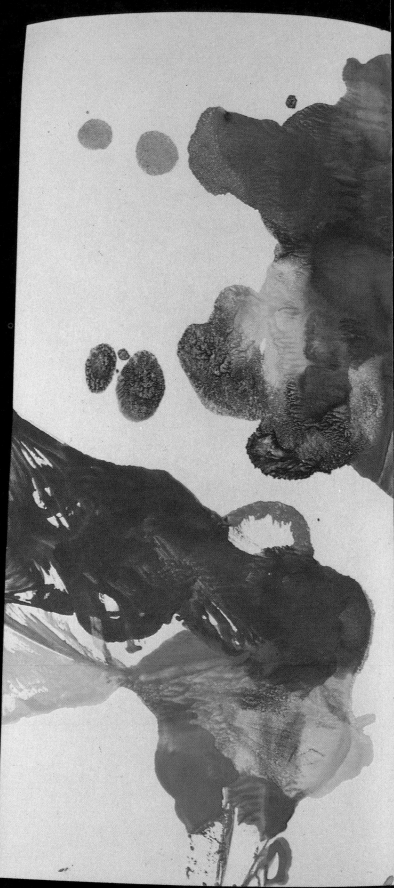

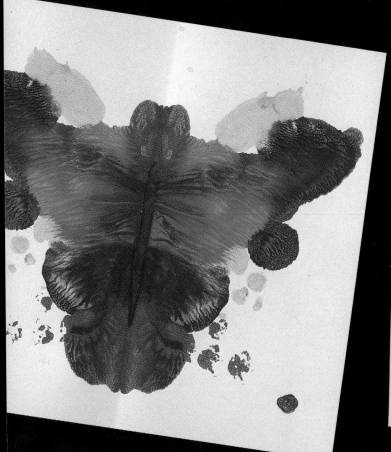

▲ Fold a sheet of paper in half and then open out flat again.

Dip some lengths of string in runny paint and lay them on one side of the paper with the ends hanging over the edge.

Try to make interesting shapes with the string.

Fold the paper over along the original fold and smooth over with your hand.

Put one hand firmly on top of the folded paper and pull the ends of the string out with the other hand.

Unfold the paper and you will find two identical swirly patterns.

If you don't want the colors to mix together, lay one piece of string down at a time and allow the paint to dry before using the next color.

▶ Wax and paint do not mix but you can get some interesting effects by using them together. Make simple patterns on a sheet of paper with a wax crayon. Paint over the pattern with runny paint. The paint will not stay where the wax marks are!

▼ Look for something that has an interesting texture – the bark of a tree, a piece of rough wood, or some bumpy glass. Tape a piece of paper over the textured surface and carefully rub with a wax crayon.

Paint over the wax pattern with runny paint.

▶ Draw a picture or make a pattern with colored wax crayons. Using a thick brush and fairly runny paint, cover the whole picture. The wax crayons will show through leaving a painted background to your picture.

▼ Color a sheet of paper with different colored wax crayons – there shouldn't be any white paper showing! Paint over the wax with thick black paint – you may need several layers – and leave to dry.

Scrape some of the paint away with the back of a spoon or the end of a pencil. The wax crayon will show through where you scrape the paint away.

Try making patterns with vegetables and paint! Look for vegetables with interesting textures.

Start with a carrot. You can slice the carrot across the middle or lengthwise. Dip the cut surface in some thick paint and press onto a sheet of paper.

Cut a potato in half. You can either scoop out a pattern in the cut surface or, using a knife, cut away a section to leave a raised pattern. Dip the potato halves in thick paint and print onto paper. A cabbage cut in quarters also makes a good print.

Try experimenting with different vegetables cut in different ways.

PASTE PAINT

Paste Recipe
1. Measure out a cup of flour and 3 cups of water.
2. In a saucepan, mix a little of the water with the flour to make a smooth paste.
3. Add the rest of the water and ask a grown-up to heat the mixture until it boils – they must keep stirring all the time! Turn the heat down and let the mixture simmer until the paste thickens.

When the paste is cold, spoon a little into some small containers. Add some paint to each container and mix well.

Cut out some pieces of cardboard to use as scrapers. Try cutting notches in the end of one piece to make an interesting shape.

Cover a piece of paper with paste paint using a thick brush.

Using cardboard scrapers, scrape away areas of the paste paint. Try making different marks by using different sizes of scrapers.

PAINTED FRAMES

By now, you should have lots of patterns and pictures that need framing! Or, you might want to make frames for your postcards and photographs.

First cut some frames from pieces of cardboard. Make sure that the inside of the frame is slightly smaller than the picture you want to frame.

If you start with a small frame and then glue a slightly larger one on top and a slightly larger one on top of that, you will get a layered effect.

Try using methods like spattering, wax and paint, and paste paint to decorate your frames.

If you want to use paste paint, glue the painted paper onto the card before you cut out the frame.

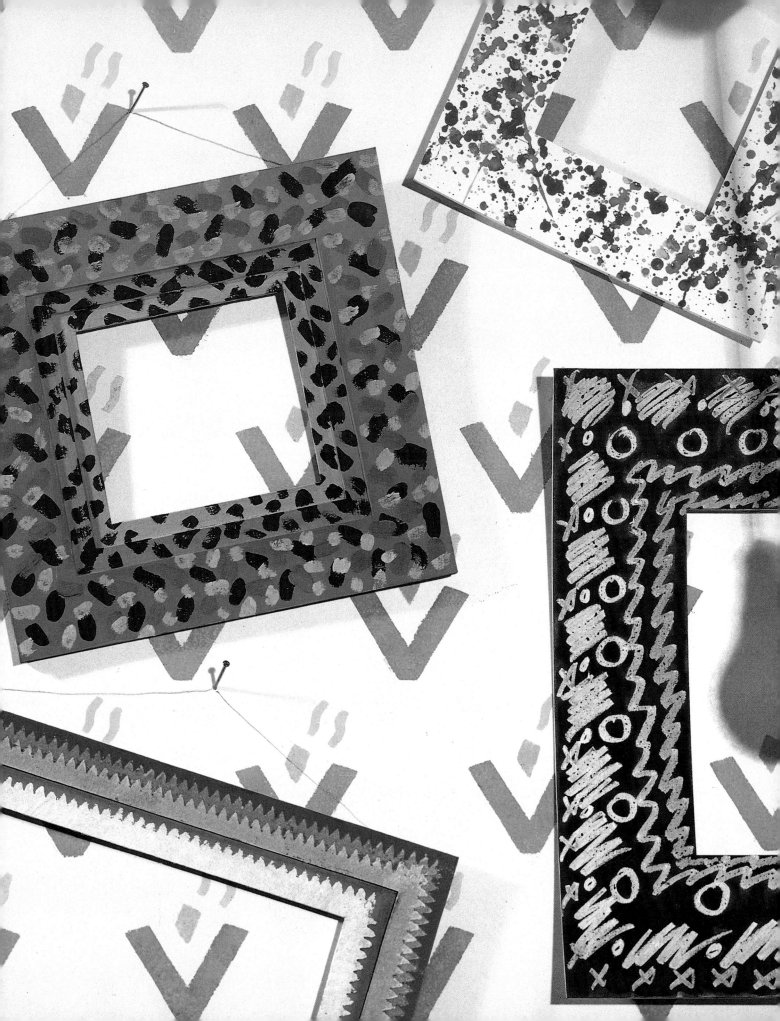

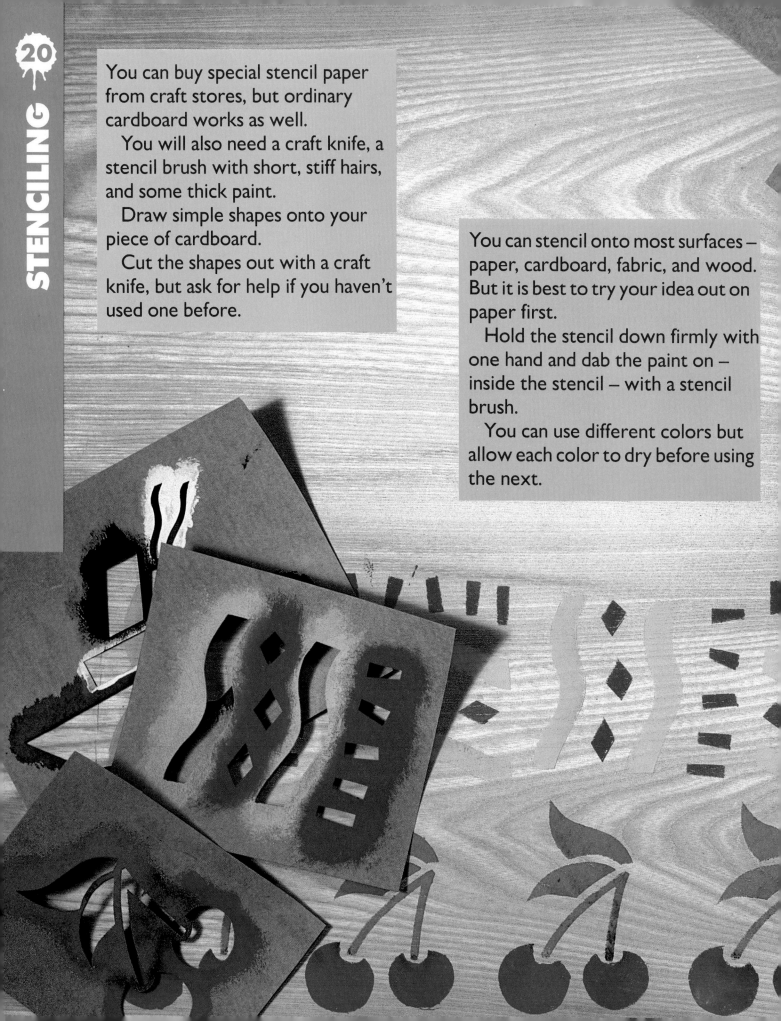

You can buy special stencil paper from craft stores, but ordinary cardboard works as well.

You will also need a craft knife, a stencil brush with short, stiff hairs, and some thick paint.

Draw simple shapes onto your piece of cardboard.

Cut the shapes out with a craft knife, but ask for help if you haven't used one before.

You can stencil onto most surfaces – paper, cardboard, fabric, and wood. But it is best to try your idea out on paper first.

Hold the stencil down firmly with one hand and dab the paint on – inside the stencil – with a stencil brush.

You can use different colors but allow each color to dry before using the next.

Not all Easter eggs are made of chocolate! These eggs have been hard-boiled and decorated with wax crayons, candle wax, food coloring, and onion skins!

Always ask for help when boiling the eggs and make sure they are cold before you decorate them.

Treat the eggs gently when you are decorating them or they will crack!

Onion Skin Eggs

Wrap an egg in layers of onion skins. Put the egg and onion skins onto a piece of fabric or into the toe of an old pair of stockings and tie up the bundle. Hard-boil the egg. When the water is cool take the egg out and unwrap it. It will be beautifully marbled in an orange-brown color.

Wax and Dye Eggs 1
Draw a pattern on an egg (before hard-boiling) with a white wax crayon or a piece of candle. Don't press too hard!

Put a few drops of food coloring into some water in a saucepan. Ask a grown-up to hardboil the egg in it. When the egg is cooked, take it out and leave it to cool. The food coloring colors the egg in the places where there is no wax.

Wax and Dye Eggs 2
For this method, you must ask a grown-up to help with dripping the wax onto the egg and using the oven!

Light a candle and let blobs of wax drop onto the egg. Put some food coloring and water into a saucer and gently roll the egg around. Drop some more candle wax onto the egg and roll it around in a saucer of darker food coloring and water.

Put the egg on a baking dish in a medium-hot oven. After a few minutes, take the egg out and wipe off any excess wax.

If it's raining outside, why not paint a sunny scene on your window! Or, you could make a pattern over the whole window.

Use quite thick poster paint and paint straight
onto the glass. The paint will wash off
easily when you want to change your scene.

The plates, knives, forks, and spoons on the tablecloth may look real, but you can't pick them up because they are painted on.

If you use special fabric paints and pens – from craft stores – you can wash the fabric over and over and the paint won't come out!

It helps to put a piece of cardboard under the area you are painting to keep the fabric steady.

Fabric pens are good for doing outlines and detailed work, but use paints and a fat brush for larger areas.

Most fabric paints should be left to dry and then ironed — but always read the instructions carefully and ask a grown-up for help using the iron.

With the help of special face paints and makeup, you can make yourself look completely different in a matter of minutes!

Try not to rub your arms or legs together when you have painted them as this may smudge the colors.

Make a rough drawing of what you want to look like on a piece of paper and keep this beside you when you are painting yourself.

Useful Hints

- ● Tie your hair back.

- ● Don't wear anything with a high neck.

- ● Only use special face paints or makeup. Don't use ordinary paints or markers.

- ● Use the largest mirror you can find.

- ● If you find it difficult to paint your own face, ask a friend to help.

- ● Put newspaper on the dressing table or floor.

- ● Face paints will come off easily with cleansing cream, moist tissues, or soap and water.

Marbling is not difficult to do and you can use marbled papers for writing on or for wrapping gifts or covering books. Every sheet will look different!

Find a baking dish at least 1″ high (2.5cm) and large enough to hold the size of paper you want to marble.

Fill the dish almost to the top with water and add a few drops of vinegar.

Drop small amounts of any oil-based paint onto the surface of the water and swirl them around with a stick, pencil, or cardboard comb.

Hold opposite ends of a clean sheet of paper and lay it on the surface of the water. Try to make sure there are no air bubbles. Gently lift the paper off and put it – colored side up – on some newspaper to dry.

On the next page you can see some of the different effects you can get. Try making more than one print from the same paints.